STORY TALK 3

Sheila Freeman and Esther Munns

Nelson

CONTENTS

Picking up clues

If at first you do not see

Story talk

Once upon a time

PICTURE CLUES – HUMPHREY'S DIARY

This *Story Talk* starts with all sorts of adventures. Meet a kite-flying mouse, a supercat, a proud princess, dragons of death and disaster, and two extraordinary knights on strange quests. You will have read about heroes and heroines before; pick up the clues to discover what is unusual about this bunch.

First, let us introduce you to Humphrey, a church mouse who keeps a diary. Here, and on the following two pages, you will find some entries and pictures from *The diary of a Church Mouse* by Graham Oakley.

They are mixed up because a nosy mouse tried to read the diary, dropped it and the pages fell out! You are going to put the diary back in order.

18th–25th March

7th March

Blow the world, it just isn't ready for my ideas. I wash my hands of it. Posterity will know where to lay the blame.

We went out in the fields and flew our kites today. It struck me as I watched them that Progress has turned its back on kites. What they need is for some Great Genius to come and drag them into the twentieth century. Come to think of it I'm not doing anything myself for the next few weeks.

4

2nd March

17th March

Four days of inspired work and I've altered the course of Kite History. I've given civilisation its first acrobatic kite!

Enthusiastic interest shown in my new kite.

31st March

No sleep. I am creating the Ultimate Kite. Tomorrow the world will be astounded.

26th March

Worked night and day on revolutionary new kite. Because of rain and dull weather, morale is at a low ebb in the vestry but my new kite will put the colour back into their drab lives.

Everybody forced to take notice of new kite.

8th–16th March

4th–6th March

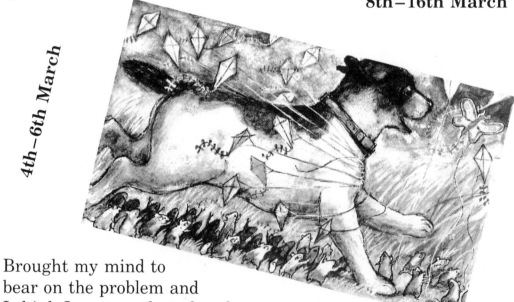

Brought my mind to bear on the problem and I think I can say that already I have taken a great stride for mankind, kitewise.

6

New kite attracted
a gigantic amount
of attention.

27th–30th March

In pairs, look at and talk about all the clues which will help you to put the entries and pictures in a sensible order.

There are *nine* entries and only *six* pictures. Decide which entries will be without illustrations.

When you are ready, write out the dates on a sheet of paper, one below the other but leaving space in between. Underneath each date, write the first few words of the entry you think goes with that date. Add a few words of your own to describe any picture you have chosen to go with that entry.

Join up with another pair. Share your ideas. Are their words and pictures in the same order as yours? Which entries haven't got any pictures? Do you all agree? Talk about any changes you might want to make and why.

Look again at the pictures. Can you spot Humphrey in each of them?

7

PICTURE CLUES – SUPERCAT SAMPSON

Look carefully at these six pictures which come from near the beginning of *The Church Mice in action*, another story about Humphrey and his friends and Sampson, the cat.

8

2

Use the title of the book and the clues in all the pictures to write
your own adventure story about Supercat Sampson.
    You will need to think about:

- names for your characters and what kinds of people or creatures
  they are;

- where the story takes place;

- an exciting beginning that will make your readers want to read on;

- where the pictures will come in your story.

9

When you are pleased with your story and have copied out your best effort, give it a title.

Swap your story with a friend.

Find a copy of *The Church Mice in action* to see what Graham Oakley wrote and how he uses pictures to help tell his story.

The Church Mice also appear in many other stories by the same author. Here is a list of titles: *The Church Mouse*; *The Church Mice spread their wings*; *The Church Mice adrift*; *The Church Mice at Christmas*; *The Church Mice at bay*; *The Church Cat abroad*.

Make a big poster for the book corner, advertising the *Church Mice* books. You could cut out words, letters, numbers and pictures from catalogues, newspapers, packets and all kinds of everyday print.

The ransom note picture (number 5) may give you some ideas for your poster.

PICKING UP CLUES

The editor of the *Wortlethorpe Clarion* has asked one of his reporters to interview Supercat Sampson about his big win. Work in pairs, one of you playing the part of the reporter, the other taking the role of Sampson.

Make a notebook out of scrap paper and jot down a list of questions for the reporter to ask Sampson.

The reporter will need to make a few notes as Supercat talks. Some of you might be able to tape-record the interview instead of making notes.

Work together to write the story "Supercat Sampson wins fortune". Look at the newspaper picture (number 1) again to see how to set out your news story.

FOLK AND FAIRY STORIES - PETRONELLA

In groups, look carefully at the illustrations on this page.

On a large sheet of paper make a list of all the stories and poems they remind you of.

3

Characters	Are usually	Are not often
Princes		
Princesses	kind, beautiful, good, helpless	ugly, clever
Kings	old	
Dragons	fierce	
Cats		
Knights		
Frogs		
Step-mothers		

Choose one of the stories you remember well. Jot down the names of the characters and the main happenings in the story.

Practise telling your story round your group. You will need to decide how to begin, where another person will take over the storytelling and how to end. Your aim should be to keep your listeners interested all the time.

Share your stories with other groups in the class.

What did you find out about some of the characters in your stories?
   Copy and complete a chart like the one we have started on the opposite page.

Talk about how princesses in fairy stories usually behave. Now meet Princess Petronella . . .

In the kingdom of Skyclear Mountain, three princes were always born to the king and queen. The oldest prince was always called Michael, the middle prince was always called George, and the youngest was always called Peter. When they were grown, they always went out to seek their fortunes. What happened to the oldest prince and the middle prince no one ever knew. But the youngest prince always rescued a princess, brought her home, and in time ruled over the kingdom. That was the way it had always been. And so far as anyone knew, that was the way it would always be.

What clues are there at the beginning of this story to tell us that we might be in for a surprise?
   What do you think the next paragraph will tell us? Read on!

   Until now.
   Now was the time of King Peter the twenty-sixth and Queen Blossom. An oldest prince was born, and a middle prince. But the youngest prince turned out to be a girl.

15

"Well," said the king gloomily, "we can't call her Peter. We'll have to call her Petronella. And what's to be done about it, I'm sure I don't know."

There was nothing to be done. The years passed, and the time came for the princes to go out and seek their fortunes. Michael and George said good-bye to the king and queen and mounted their horses. Then out came Petronella. She was dressed in travelling clothes, with her bag packed and a sword by her side.

"If you think," she said, "that I'm going to sit at home, you are mistaken. I'm going to seek my fortune, too."

"Impossible!" said the king.

"What will people say?" cried the queen.

"Look," said Prince Michael, "be reasonable, Pet. Stay home.

Sooner or later a prince will turn up here."

Petronella smiled. She was a tall, handsome girl with flaming red hair and when she smiled in that particular way it meant she was trying to keep her temper.

"I'm going with you," she said. "I'll find a prince if I have to rescue one from something myself. And that's that."

The grooms brought out her horse, she said good-bye to her parents, and away she went behind her two brothers.

They travelled into the flatlands below Skyclear Mountain. After many days, they entered a great dark forest. They came to a place where the road divided into three, and there at the fork sat a little, wrinkled old man covered with dust and spiderwebs.

Talk about what might happen next in the story. Here are some things to think about:

- Who is the little old man? Will he be of help to them or not?
- Will Prince Michael, Prince George and Petronella stay together, or will they each take a separate road?
- Will Petronella find a prince? If so, how and where will she find him? Will she have to rescue him? If so, from what or whom and how will she do it?
- If she does not find a prince, what will happen to her?
- How will the story end?

Remember the clues you have already picked up which suggest that this is a rather *unusual* fairy story . . .

Make a plan of your story, then write it out.

Read your story to another group in the class.

If you want to know what really happened to Petronella, read *The practical princess* by Jay Williams.

FOLK AND FAIRY STORIES - TUMBLEWEED

Look closely at the title and the front cover of this book.

Write a few sentences to describe Sir Tumbleweed as he is shown on the cover. How do you think he got his name? What clues tell us that he is not the sort of knight we usually find in fairy stories?

Read how the author, Dick King-Smith, describes his hero.

Sir Tumbleweed was a tall thin knight, with bright red hair and a long red moustache that drooped sadly at either end. Of all the knights in Merrie England, he was the most accident-prone. He was also a very nervous man. For instance, he was scared of horses. They were so large (they had to be, to carry knights in heavy armour) that once he was mounted (hoisted aboard by block and tackle) he seemed to be a frighteningly long way from the ground. Being scared of heights, Sir Tumbleweed would throw his armoured arms around the animal's neck. Off would go the startled horse, and off would come Sir Tumbleweed. Once down, he could not get up, and many a lonely hour he spent lying on the ground shouting "Help!" inside his helmet.

In groups, talk about any differences you notice between your descriptions and the author's.

Towards the middle of the book we find that Tumbleweed has become a very different person, with the help of Arthur the lion and Spearhead the unicorn.

Sir Tumbleweed's fame spread about the country like wildfire and, as the story passed from one to another, so it grew.

This red-haired giant of a knight, tall as a tree, had flown – yes flown – into the Greate Meadowe on a winged white beast as swift as an arrow. He has tipped the mighty Sir Basil the Beastly off his charger with one prod of his finger, then sliced him into small pieces. Finally, when a hundred, nay two hundred knights had dared to confront him, he had called to his aid a gigantic man-eating lion!

It was not surprising, therefore, that as Sir Tumbleweed and his two companions moved about the countryside, everyone gave them a wide berth.

The mere sight of the fearsome warrior approaching sent peasants scuttling for their huts and hovels, and any gentleman who espied the terrible trio seemed suddenly to remember some pressing business in the opposite direction.

All this was bad for Sir Tumbleweed.

His victory in the Tournament and the routing of the other knights (for both of which he now gave himself the credit rather than the unicorn and the lion), combined with the awe in which he was so plainly held, went to his head. It swelled, and his behaviour became hard to bear.

He would shout insults at any knight they chanced to meet, calling him rude names like "Sir Potbelly" or "Sir Bigbum", and when the rider made off, rather than face the fabled might of the Champion, Sir Tumbleweed would jeer at him. "Cowardy cowardy custard, wouldn't eat the mustard!" he would shout, with a self-satisfied grin on his once gloomy face. Even his moustache began to look different, for he had taken to brushing the ends of it upwards in a fierce fashion.

21

It was plain to Arthur and Spearhead that the knight had grown much too big for his boots, and needed taking down a peg if he were not to become quite unbearable. They discussed the matter while Sir Tumbleweed slept.

"What he needs," said Spearhead, "is a short sharp shock."

"Like fighting for his life . . ." said Arthur.

"Without us to help him . . ." said Spearhead.

"Against something really terrifying . . ." said Arthur.

"A dragon for example . . ."

"Yes, a simply huge fire-breathing one . . ."

"With great leathery wings . . ."

"And a long lashing tail . . ."

"And terrible claws . . ."

"And horrible teeth!"

"Right," said Spearhead. "That's settled."

"That'll teach him to be so cocky," said Arthur.

Both animals thought with pleasure about this plan, in a silence broken only by Sir Tumbleweed's snores and a little scratching noise somewhere nearby, the sort of noise a cat makes sharpening its claws on a tree.

"That only leaves us one thing to do then," said Spearhead.

"Yes," said Arthur. "We need to find a nice fierce dragon."

"That might be arranged," said a low pleasant voice in the darkness of the windy night.

Make a list of the ways in which Tumbleweed has changed.

Now each of you choose a different character from this list:
- a traveller from another part of the country;
- a knight who was once a friend of Tumbleweed;
- a knight who has been defeated in the tournament;
- the wife of Sir Basil the Beastly;
- a peasant man, woman or child.

Think of a suitable name for yourself.
Talk about the sort of person you are and the work you do.
Each of you tell the story of how you first met Tumbleweed.
Where were you and what were you doing? How did Tumbleweed behave then? What do you think of him now?

In threes, write a short play called "A conversation between the lion, the unicorn, and a dragon", in which Arthur, Spearhead and a dragon plan how to stop Sir Tumbleweed from becoming too big-headed.
The last part of the extract on page 22 will help you, but try to write some of the conversation in your own words. Give the dragon more to say. Add as much extra detail of your own as you can.

Before you begin:
Read again all the parts of the story you have been given.
Remind yourselves how plays should be written down.
Start with Arthur and Spearhead talking. Bring the dragon in later.
Think about how to end your play.

When the play is finished, each of you choose to be one of the characters and learn your part.
Think about how you can use your voices to build up a frightening picture of the dragon.

When you have written and practised your short play, you could use it to introduce the book *Tumbleweed* to another class.

A PAIR OF DRAGONS - THE DRAGON OF DEATH

In a faraway, faraway forest
lies a treasure of infinite worth,
but guarding it closely forever
looms a being as old as the earth.

Its body is big as a boulder
and armoured with shimmering scales,
even the mountaintops tremble
when it thrashes its seven great tails.

Its eyes tell a story of terror,
they gleam with an angry red flame
as it timelessly watches its riches,
and the dragon of death is its name.

Its teeth are far sharper than daggers,
they can tear hardest metal to shreds.
It has seven mouths filled with these weapons,
for its neck swells to seven great heads.

Each head is as fierce as the other,
Each head breathes a fiery breath,
and any it touches must perish,
set ablaze by the dragon of death.

All who have foolishly stumbled
on the dragon of death's golden cache*
remain evermore in that forest,
nothing left of their bodies but ash.

* "cache" is another word for hidden treasure

24

Read the poem, or listen to it being read to you.

Make a list of the words from the poem which will help you draw a picture of the dragon.

On a large piece of paper draw the dragon as it is described in the poem.

In groups or as a whole class, plan how you could read the poem aloud in an interesting way.
   You will need to decide:
which verses to say all together or in small groups;
which lines or verses might sound better read by one person;
which lines to read more loudly and which lines to read more softly;
which lines to read slowly and which lines to read quickly.

Try out lots of different ways, then write out a plan like the one below.
   This is our suggestion on how to begin the poem, but you will have your own ideas.

The dragon of death	*Voice 1* – slowly, clearly stressing the words **dragon** and **death**
Verse 1 In a faraway, faraway forest lies a treasure of infinite worth, but guarding it closely forever looms a being as old as the earth.	*Group 1* – very quietly, slowly and mysteriously *Group 2* – join in – still slowly but gradually getting louder; make the word "looms" into a long sounding word

A PAIR OF DRAGONS - THE UNPREPARED DRAGON

All dragons aren't the same. They don't all look alike and they certainly don't all behave like the dragon of death. Imagine a dragon who has never fought a knight before.

Here are some illustrations to help you build up a picture of the kind of dragon he is.

Copy these pictures.

Make up a story to go with the pictures and write it out underneath them.

You might like to show the dragon speaking in your pictures. Do this by drawing a speech bubble beside the dragon's mouth, and writing the words inside the bubble, like this:

CHOOSE YOUR OWN ADVENTURE

"Tumbleweed meets a dragon" is the title of your story. In groups, decide whether he meets "The dragon of death" or "The unprepared dragon" (see pages 24–25 and pages 26–27). Here are some questions you will need to answer as you plan your story. Jot down your answers on a large sheet of paper.

What is your dragon doing before Tumbleweed arrives on the scene?
1 Talking to someone? If so, to whom and what about?
2 Thinking about his next meal? If so, describe his favourite meal.
3 Worried about something? If so, what is his problem?
4 Something **you** decide.

How does your dragon behave when he first sees Tumbleweed?
1 Run away? If so, where to? Describe the dragon's hiding place.
2 Try to look fierce even though he is frightened? If so, what does he do and what is he thinking?
3 Sharpen his claws in readiness for his dinner? If so, what does he say to Tumbleweed as he does this?
4 As **you** decide.

What do they do next?
1 Swap adventure stories? If so, write the adventure story each one tells.
2 Arrange a party for their friends? If so, write a letter of invitation and make up a game to play at the party.
3 Agree to fight? If so, draw up a list of rules and describe the contest.
4 Anything **you** decide.

How does your story end? Write your group story.

Read *Tumbleweed* to find out what kind of dragon the author chose for his knight to encounter.

HENRY'S QUEST

The front cover of a book may look interesting but sometimes it is difficult to tell exactly what the story inside the cover is going to be about.

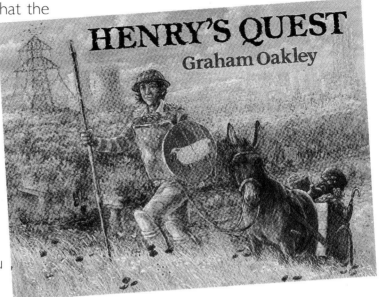

In pairs, look closely at the details on this front cover:

Talk about everything you notice – try not to miss anything.

Make a note of the things you find.

List the questions you hope will be answered when you read the story.

What do you already know that might help you guess what this book is about? For example:

- Have you read any other "quest" stories? Are there any in this chapter?

- What do you know about people who carry shields? Do they usually ride donkeys and wear cricket pads?

- Do you recognise any of the buildings in the background of the picture? What is strange about them?

- What kinds of stories does Graham Oakley usually write and draw? Look back to pages 4–11.

Share your ideas with others in the class. Help each other to make guesses about the answers to the questions you have written down. Now look at the **back cover** to find out what Henry's Quest is.

Henry's Quest is to find Petrol.
But what does it look like?

ISBN 0-333-40841-1

Why do you think he doesn't know what Petrol looks like?
Do you think the story will take place mainly in the past, the present or the future? Give reasons for your choice.

Read or listen to the description of the story from the **inside cover.**

Henry is a shepherd in a small country ruled by a king.

One day, the king – who is keen on knights and chivalry – announces a Quest, with the hand of his daughter as the reward for success.

The Quest is to find Petrol, a magical substance which alone can make the king's shiny metal heirlooms on wheels move. Henry has no clear idea of what Petrol looks like. Which makes the Quest rather difficult.

But Henry is not deterred: he harnesses his donkey, Frederick, to a cart holding the things a knight might need when on a Quest, and sets off – to meet with some of the strangest adventures a knight has ever had to contend with.

Graham Oakley, author/illustrator of the famous *Church Mice* books, has created an enthralling story of an extraordinary world.

Have any of your questions been answered now?

If there are any words you still do not understand when you have talked with your partner, ask your teacher for help or look up the words in a dictionary.

In groups, write your own story called "Henry's Quest". But before you go into groups, the whole class should agree about:

- the kind of hero Henry is;

- the time in which his adventure takes place;

- some of the places Henry might visit on his quest (e.g. a deserted coal mine, a village by a lake, etc.).

First make a copy of the decisions made by the whole class.

Each group should then plan and write one adventure for Henry in which he thinks he has found Petrol but then discovers it is something else. Add some drawings if you wish.

When all the groups have finished writing their adventures, read them aloud. Decide as a class what order to put the stories in. Write a few sentences to link one adventure with the next.

IF AT FIRST YOU DO NOT SEE

WOULD YOU RATHER...?

There is no right answer to questions which begin with these words. If at first you do not see why your friends would rather be lost in a desert than in a crowd, listen to their reasons. Try to understand how they feel.

Would you rather be made to eat . . .

spider stew

slug dumplings   mashed worms   or drink snail squash

On your own, choose what *you* would rather be made to eat or drink. Be ready to say why.

In small groups listen to what everyone has chosen. Begin by saying "I would rather ... because ...".

Do not argue with each other. Try to understand how other children feel. Remember there is no right answer to the question "Would *you* rather?".

Make up some more "Would you rather?" questions to try out on your friends.

Here are some more which you will find in John Burningham's picture book *Would you rather?*

Would you rather your house was surrounded by

- water
- snow
- or jungle?

Would you rather be lost

- in the fog
- at sea
- in a desert
- in a forest
- or in a crowd?

In pairs, talk about a time when you had to choose between one thing and another and you found it hard. It might have been at school or at home.

Listen carefully to each other's stories.

33

TWO MONSTERS

These two monsters have a problem.

One monster lives on the west side of a mountain, the other lives on the east side.

They speak to each other through a hole in the mountain but they can't see each other.

One evening the first monster called through the hole, "Can you see how beautiful it is? Day is departing."

"Day departing?" called back the second monster. "You mean night arriving, you twit!"

They become more and more annoyed and throw stones, boulders and rocks at each other.

"You're a hairy, overstuffed, empty-headed, boss-eyed mess!" shouted the first monster as he threw yet another massive boulder.

"You're a pathetic, addlebrained, smelly, lily-livered custard tart!" screamed the second monster hurling a yet larger rock.

In pairs, make up some more angry conversation as the two monsters go on shouting at each other.

Write down your conversation and read it aloud.

Later in the story, after they have smashed down the mountain, the monsters see each other for the first time. It is sunset.

Draw a picture of the two monsters looking at the sunset.

Under your picture write what the monsters say to each other.

What do you think their problem was?

How would you have helped them solve it?

In your class, think about how you could share the ideas in this story for a school assembly.

First of all talk about the arguments you have at home or at school because you do not see "eye to eye" with your family or friends.

Write down some of them.

In pairs, act out one of the quarrels. How will you end your argument? When you are ready, share your work with the rest of the class. Talk about the problem that led to the quarrel and suggest ways of solving it. Could the quarrel have been avoided?

You could call your assembly "If at first you do not see".

A WALK IN THE PARK

Writers and artists want us to look very closely at their words *and* their illustrations because often there are messages in the illustrations that are not in the words. Look at this picture from *A walk in the park* by Anthony Browne.

Both dogs were free.

If you look at this park quickly you might see only the dogs chasing each other because the words tell us that is what is happening. Now look again more carefully.

In pairs talk about all the unusual things happening in the park.

Can you think of any reasons why the artist has put them in his picture but has not written about them?

They chased each other all over the park.

37

Draw or trace these shapes.

Talk about what each could be thinking and saying. Write one or two sentences inside each square and each bubble.
   How many different ideas did your class come up with?

Later in the story . . . . .

Albert felt too hot, so to cool himself he plunged into the fountain.

Work in pairs. One of you should close your book and draw the fountain on a large sheet of paper as your partner describes it to you.
   When your partner's description is not clear, ask a question.

After you have done your best, look at Anthony Browne's fountain. Is yours anything like it?
   Did you have to ask many questions? If so, what were they about?

Work with your partner now. Remember how difficult it was for you to describe and draw the fountain.

Together, write a clear description so that someone who has not seen the picture could draw it. Try it out at home and share the fun with your family.

Plan and draw your own everyday object so that it looks "real" until you look at it closely.

Here are some ideas:

- a piece of furniture;
- a machine;
- a ride at a fairground;
- a well-known building.

Describe the object to friends and see how accurate their drawings are.

See how many Anthony Browne books you can find to talk about and enjoy.

LETTERS TO COLOURS

Have you ever thought of colours being like friends you could write to?

Read two of "Lettie's letters to colours" from *Letters for Lettie* by John Agard.

Among her birthday presents Lettie had a painting set with plenty different colours. Some of these colours she had never heard of before – colours with strange-sounding names like sienna and indigo and buff.

Suppose the whole world was only one colour, thought Lettie as she played around with the different colours, making squiggles here and squiggles there.

Just imagine all the birds being one colour and flying around in a sky which was the same green as the grass or the same brown as the earth. And everywhere all over the world everybody had the same colour hair, the same colour eyes, the same colour skin.

That wouldn't be very nice, thought Lettie. She wouldn't like to look down at the grass, then look up at the sky, and find the same colour staring back at her.

No, she would much rather have a world with plenty colours like her painting set, even if some of the colours did have funny names.

But this morning, as Lettie sat there playing with her painting set, her head wasn't only filled with colours. She was thinking of other things as well, and those other things, as you can guess, were her letters.

And as she made shapes of colour on the page, she thought how wonderful it would be writing letters to colours as if they were friends. After all, aren't friends supposed to liven you up and make you feel bright?

"Well, that's exactly what colours are for," said Lettie aloud, going straight to her writing pad and pen.

Now, which colour shall I pick first?

Lettie didn't take long to make up her mind, for the first thing through the window that caught her eye was the sky.

So Lettie began a letter to blue.

Dear blue,

Up there in the sky you look like a nice clean sheet. I could cover myself with you. I'm telling you true, blue.

Lettie felt so pleased with this letter, especially with the little rhyme at the end, that she couldn't wait to begin writing to green.

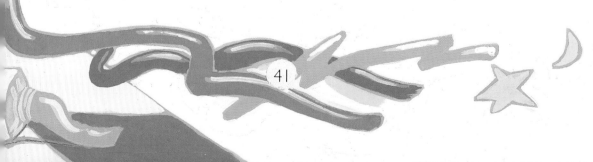

Write a letter beginning "Dear green", but think about a particular kind of green and what it reminds you of before you begin to write your letter.

You could write a letter to more than one colour, as Lettie did when she wrote to yellow, black and white.

Team together with others in the class who have written a letter to the same colour as you have. Think of interesting ways of displaying your letters and celebrating your colour.

THE PAINTING

In this poem Ruth, aged eleven, remembers how she felt when her teacher questioned her about the colours she had used in her painting.

I am sure the world would
be a better place
If soil was pink
Or some bright new colour
And grass was purple,
And sheep were blue
And the sky was made of real silver,
And the sun of real gold,
And the trees were white with green tentacles;

This is my painting.

But behind that tree is someone,
Someone who is going to make me angry.
Because in a minute that someone will,
Make the soil brown,
The grass green,
The sheep a dirty white,
The sky blue,
And the sun yellow.
That someone is my teacher.
Does she not know I was only
Making the world gay?

Tell each other stories about a time when you got angry because somebody wanted to change the way you were seeing or doing something.

BIRD AND BOY

A boy wants to fly. He talks to a bird about his wish.

In groups, make a list of all the good things and the bad things the bird might have to say about flying.

We have given you a flying start!

Good points	Bad points
● My air is fresh and free from petrol fumes.	● There are noisy, frightening metal birds flying in my sky.
● Flying, I see the tops of mountains.	● Sometimes the air is very cold.

Read or listen to the poem "Bird and Boy" by Leslie Norris.

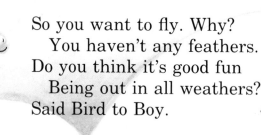

So you want to fly. Why?
    You haven't any feathers.
Do you think it's good fun
    Being out in all weathers?
Said Bird to Boy.

You haven't any wings,
    You can't build a nest.
Why aren't you satisfied.
    With the things you do best?
Said Bird to Boy.

What would it be like?
    A sky full of boys,
Their arms flapping, their big feet –
    And the noise!
Said Bird to Boy.

44

Have you ever tried perching
    In some old tree
When it's snowing? It's not funny,
    Believe me!
Said Bird to Boy.

Be comfortable, do your own thing,
    Your skateboard, your bike,
Your football, all the other
    Things you like.
        Why try to fly?
    Stay out of the sky,
Said Bird to Boy.

    Yes, you're right, I can't just
        Flap my arms and fly.
    But I dream about it often,
        Winging through the sky,
    Above the houses, the streets.
        I'd like to try.
    Said Boy to Bird.

With a partner, pick out all the reasons why the bird doesn't think the boy would enjoy flying.

Draw the bird's reasons inside *seven* picture frames with words from the poem under each one. Here are two examples:

"You haven't any feathers"   "Out in all weathers"

Look again at the last verse. Talk about the boy's dream. What things would he be able to *see*, *feel* and *hear* as he was flying? Jot down all your thoughts.

On your own, use some of the ideas to write a poem called "Winging through the sky".

Draw a picture to go with your writing.

In small groups, try several ways of reading "Bird and Boy" aloud. Choose one way and practise it for sharing with other groups. See how quickly you can learn the poem.

46

"I'D LIKE TO TRY"

In this poem, Leslie Norris looks at flying from the boy's point of view. Read it aloud, or quietly to yourself.

Flying,
   He saw the earth flat as a plate,
   As if there were no hills, as if houses
   Were only roofs, as if the trees
   Were only the leaves that covered
   The treetops. He could see the shadows
   The clouds cast when they sailed over the fields,
   He could see the river like the silver track
   Left by a snail, and roads narrow as ribbons.

   He could not see Mickey French next door,
   In bed with a cold, nor his two sisters
   Playing "Happy Families" as they watched
   The television. He could not see his kitten.

Flying,
   He felt the air as solid as water
   When he spread his fingers against it.
   He felt it cool against his face, he felt
   His hair whipped. He felt weightless
   As if he were hollow, he felt the sun
   Enormously bright and warm on his back,
   He felt his eyes watering. He felt
   The small, moist drops the clouds held.

   He could not feel the grass, he could not
   Feel the rough stones of the garden wall.
   He could not remember the harsh, dry bark
   Of the apple tree against his knees.

Flying,
   He could hear the wind hissing, the note
   Changed when he turned his head. He heard
   His own voice when he sang. Very faintly,
   He heard the school bus as it grumbled
   Past the church, he thought he could hear
   The voices of the people as they shouted
   In amazement when they saw him swoop and glide.

   He could not hear the birds sing, nor the chalk
   Squeak against the blackboard, nor the mower
   As it whirred along, nor the clock tick.
   He could not hear the bacon sizzle in the pan,
   He could not hear his friend calling him.

When you have read the poem several times, copy and complete this chart of what the boy sees, feels and hears.

Sees	How or when he sees it
the earth	flat as a plate
Feels	**How or when he feels it**
the air	as solid as water
Hears	**How or when he hears it**
the school bus	as it grumbled past the church

Imagine that you are the boy or girl who is flying. You are taking part in a live television programme. Describe what you see, feel and hear as you fly over the place you live in and the school you go to.
   This picture by Shirley Hughes should give you some ideas.

Each poem has its own pattern and shape. Look again at the poems on pages 44–45 and 47–48. What interesting things do you notice about their patterns and shapes?

THE BATTLE OF BUBBLE AND SQUEAK

Families in stories, just like families in real life, don't always agree with each other. In the Sparrow family, Mrs Alice Sparrow could not see why her children Sid, Peggy and Amy wanted to keep messy gerbils. Her husband, Bill, was pleased that Sid was willing to clear up after them.

Read or listen to the story of the Sparrow family from *The battle of Bubble and Squeak* by Philippa Pearce.

Sid may not have loved his gerbils in the way that Peggy did, but he was conscientious about them. He changed their food and water daily, and cleaned out their cage every weekend. He exercised them often. What they seemed to enjoy was the freedom of a limitless plain – the living-room table would do – with a great many tunnels. To begin with, the children made the tunnels out of newspaper rolled up, with rubber bands to keep the rolling-up in place. Then they began to collect the cardboard inner tubes of toilet rolls from the lavatory and of kitchen rolls from the kitchen. The longer tubes were kept for the table; the shorter ones went straight into the cage.

Besides using the tubes as runways, the gerbils gnawed them to bits. If they didn't gnaw cardboard, they gnawed the bars of the cage or of the restored treadmill. The cardboard they gnawed filled the cage with cardboard crumbs, and the crumbs pushed themselves out through the bars of the cage on to the table or the floor; so did the gerbil bedding. Someone had to clear up the mess. After that first night's experience, Mrs Sparrow refused to do any more clearing up after gerbils.

50

Sid did it. He used the vacuum cleaner regularly nowadays. He did not object. He rather enjoyed the job of emptying the cleaner. Once it went wrong, and he mended it.

"You can't say he doesn't work at it," said Bill Sparrow. "You might do worse than keep those gerbils, you know."

"You're soft," said Alice Sparrow. "I don't like them. I don't *trust* them."

It turned out that she was right not to trust them.

The gerbil cage was kept on the living-room table, until the table was needed. Then Sid or Peggy would lift the cage on to the wide window-sill. When the table was clear again, the cage was put back. But sometimes, of course, the children forgot to do that. It did not seem to matter much if the gerbils stayed on the window-sill, anyway. There was even room, after dark, to draw the curtains across the window, between the back of the cage and the window itself.

The curtains were rather handsome scarlet ones that Mrs Sparrow had made herself. When they were drawn behind the cage, their folds brushed against the bars at the back.

One morning Mrs Sparrow was down first, as usual, to get breakfast ready. She had raised the blind in the hall, she had brought the milk in from the doorstep, she had gone into the living-room to draw the curtains back –

There was a kind of screech from downstairs, and then the repeated screaming of "Sid! Sid! Sid!"

It was frightening.

In his school trousers and his pyjama top, Sid flew downstairs. His mother met him at the bottom of the stairs. Tears were streaming down her cheeks; she also looked

51

unspeakably angry. "Come and see what your – your THINGS have done!"

She dragged him into the living-room. The room was still in semi-darkness because the curtains had not yet been drawn back. But the gloom was shot by strong beams of light coming through two large ragged holes in the curtains. The holes were just behind the cage, and by the light through them Sid could see that the inside of the gerbil cage was littered with scraps and crumbs of scarlet. One gerbil, sitting up watchfully, seemed to be wiping its mouth free of a scarlet thread.

"They've eaten my best curtains," said Mrs Sparrow.

Peggy had followed Sid, and now Amy and Bill Sparrow were crowding to see, Amy holding tight to Bill.

Amy peeped and peered. "I didn't know gerbils ate curtains."

"They don't *eat* them," said Peggy. "They just gnaw at them."

"They've ruined them," said Mrs Sparrow.

"Can't you mend them?" asked Bill Sparrow.

"Can't *I* mend them!"

"I'll mend them," said Sid. "I'll draw the edges of the holes together. I saw you mending that tear in my duffle coat, when it had caught on the barbed wire. I'll buy red cotton exactly to match, and I'll mend it. Peggy'll help me, won't you, Peg?"

"Yes," said Peggy; "but – but –"

"But you can't," said their mother. "Your duffle coat was just torn: there was nothing missing. These curtains have been *gnawed away*. Big bits are missing, all chewed up at the bottom of those wretched creatures' cage."

"I'll do something, Mum!" cried Sid. "I could buy some more of the red stuff to patch the holes with. I've pocket money saved. I could buy you new curtains. Mum, I tell you what –"

"No," said his mother, "I'm not thinking of the curtains now."

"But, Mum, listen –"

"No," said his mother, "no, no, NO! Not another day in this house, if I can help it! They go!"

"But, Mum –"

"THEY GO!"

She would listen to no more from any of them.

That day (as her family discovered only later) Mrs Sparrow went out of her way to work to call at the newsagent's. They kept a *Wanted* and *For Sale* notice board in their window. The board was covered with postcard notices which people paid to be pinned up there for a week, or two weeks, or – rarely – three.

In small groups read again the section of the story from "One morning Mrs Sparrow was down first, as usual, to get breakfast ready ..." to "She would listen to no more from any of them".

Each of you choose different parts to read: there are five members of the Sparrow family and the storyteller.

53

Practise reading this section of the story so that it sounds like a real family quarrel.

When you are ready, you could make a tape-recording of your reading. After you have listened to it, there may be some things you would like to change. Talk about them before you try again.

Work with a partner. Choose one of the following points of view to argue about. Remember that to argue does not mean to quarrel!

1 Mrs Sparrow has a right to get rid of the gerbils because of the damage done to her curtains. What do you think?

2 Sid offered to mend the curtains, so he should have been allowed to keep the gerbils. What do you think?

3 It is wrong to advertise pets for sale in a newsagent's. What do you think?

After a little while, change sides and start to argue again.

Write the "For Sale" notice that Mrs Sparrow placed in the newsagent's.

From this part of the story, talk about what you learn about gerbils and how to look after them. What advice would you give someone who was thinking about taking the school gerbil home for the holidays? Jot down a few Do's and Don'ts.

When disaster strikes in the house of the Sparrow family, who do you think comes to the rescue of the gerbils?

Read or listen to the story to find out.

So suddenly does disaster strike.

That evening Bill Sparrow had gone to get more coal for the fire.

"Shut the back door – the draught's killing!" called Mrs Sparrow. But, as usual, Bill did not shut the door – it would

54

be so much easier to find it open when he came back, laden with coal. He pulled the back door to, but did not click it shut. It opened a little behind him as he turned away. He went off with the scuttle towards the coal-bunker.

Behind him a ginger ghost slipped up to the back door, and through it, into the house.

Ginger went through the kitchen and across the hall into the living-room. Bill Sparrow had left all those doors ajar for his return.

Once inside the living-room, Ginger melted into the shadows. The whole family were watching television. Everyone was staring, silent, in one direction. The electric light had been switched off. The fire had burnt low, but there was a cold glow from the television screen. In the light Ginger's eyes shone large, but no one saw them.

He had not chosen his time particularly well. The gerbils might so easily have been at exercise on the living-room table; but they were safely in their cage.

So at first Ginger saw nothing of particular interest. The television screen did not interest him, nor the sounds that proceeded from the set. There were gunshots, screams, alarm-bells and sirens: Ginger paid no attention.

But then there was another sound: a little scuffling and scratching, and a subdued *Creak! . . . Creak! . . . Creak!* Nobody looking at the television screen even turned a head: they were used to the fidgetings of Bubble and Squeak by now.

But the ginger ghost in the shadows began to move. From shadow to shadow he slipped, round the back of the chairs and the couch, until he was close to the table.

From inside their cage on the table the gerbils saw him. They froze.

Ginger saw them and leapt . . .

The television viewers were aware of something that

hurtled through the air, and an impact like an explosion.

That was Ginger reaching the cage. Suddenly everyone was shouting or shrieking. The cage skidded off the table and on to the floor with a crash. The whole of the barred side and roof flew off in one piece. The two gerbils leapt for their lives.

Peggy saw one gerbil and dived for it and caught it.

Ginger saw the other gerbil – Bubble – and dived for it and caught it.

Peggy was screaming because, holding one gerbil, she could do nothing about the other one. Sid was yelling because he was trying to frighten Ginger into dropping his prey. Amy was screaming, anyway. But Mrs Sparrow was not screaming. She was the only one within reach of Ginger and Bubble, and she was inspired. She flung herself forward on to Ginger's tail, gripped it, held it with both hands, hauled on it.

Ginger turned on Mrs Sparrow. He scratched her viciously: she still held on. Suddenly what was happening to him was too much to be borne – Ginger was no hero. He wanted to yowl, and he opened his mouth and yowled. A sad little bundle of fur, brindled and white, fell from his jaws. Sid saw it, darted in and picked it up.

Mrs Sparrow let go of Ginger's tail. Ginger sprang for the door – out, and across the hall and kitchen and out through the back door just as Bill Sparrow was coming in with the coal. As only a cat can, Ginger slipped between Bill's legs so that he tottered and fell, with a scuttleful of coal and a great deal of swearing.

Coal all over the kitchen floor.

Mrs Sparrow scratched quite badly.

Amy almost in hysterics.

And Bubble – "Is he all right?" whispered Peggy.

"Just," said Sid.

Bill Sparrow had left coal all over the kitchen floor and come in to see what on earth had been happening. He made his wife sit down. He switched off the television set. He reassembled the gerbil cage so that Peggy could put Squeak back. He took Amy into his arms. Then he looked at Bubble, held cupped in Sid's hands. He looked long, and then he cleared his throat. "I had a white mouse. A cat mauled it. The mouse had to be put out of its misery. It was kinder. It had to be destroyed . . ."

From her chair, Mrs Sparrow, hearing him, groaned.

57

This very exciting chapter in the book would make a good film.

In your group, choose which part of the chapter you would like to film.

Draw a storyboard for the part you have chosen, using five pictures. We have drawn the first picture for each part.

Think carefully about your pictures. The five pictures together must show, in order, what happens in that part of the chapter. But each single picture must also look interesting.

Part One

From the beginning of the chapter to where Ginger gets close to the table.

Part Two

From "From inside their cage on the table the gerbils saw him" to the part where Sid picks up Bubble.

Part Three

The last part of
the chapter.

Work in pairs. It is the next day. Imagine that you are one of the
following characters:

- Mrs Sparrow telling your neighbour what happened the night
  before;

- Ginger talking to another cat about your adventure;

- Mr Sparrow asking Sid how the accident happened after he had
  gone out to get some coal;

- Peggy telling a friend how she caught Squeak but couldn't reach
  Bubble in time.

Act out the conversation.

By the end of the story Mrs Sparrow wants to help the gerbils. What
do you think has happened to make her change her mind?

Talk about what you think happens next.

Write down all your ideas.

Choose one from your list. Write the first few lines of the next
chapter.

See how many different ways of continuing the story there are in
the class.

ANANSI, THE STORY SPIDER

Read this story from *From Tiger to Anansi* by Philip M Sherlock. Who was Anansi? He was a man and he was a spider.

Anansi's home was in the villages and forests of West Africa. From there long years ago thousands of men and women came to the islands of the Caribbean. They brought with them the stories that they loved, the stories about clever Br'er Anansi, and his friends Tiger and Crow and Moos-Moos and Kisander the cat.

Today the people of the islands still tell these stories to each other.

Here is the beginning of the story which tells us how the Tiger stories became Anansi stories.

Once upon a time and a long long time ago the Tiger was king of the forest.

At evening when all the animals sat together in a circle and talked and laughed together, Snake would ask:

"Who is the strongest of us all?"

"Tiger is strongest," cried Dog. "When Tiger whispers the trees listen. When Tiger is angry and cries out, the trees tremble.

"And who is the weakest of all?" asked Snake.

"Anansi," shouted Dog, and they all laughed together. "Anansi the spider is weakest of all. When he whispers no one listens. When he shouts everyone laughs."

Now one day the weakest and strongest came face to face, Anansi and Tiger. They met in a clearing of the forest. The frogs hiding under the cool leaves saw them. The bright-green parrots in the branches heard them.

When they met, Anansi bowed so low that his forehead touched the ground. Tiger did not greet him. Tiger just looked at Anansi.

"Good morning, Tiger," cried Anansi. "I have a favour to ask."

"And what is it, Anansi?" said Tiger.

"Tiger, we all know that you are strongest of us all. This is why we give your name to many things. We have Tiger lilies and Tiger stories and Tiger moths, and Tiger this and Tiger that. Everyone knows that I am weakest of all. This is why nothing bears my name. Tiger, let something be called after the weakest one so that men may know my name too."

"Well," said Tiger, without so much as a glance toward Anansi, "what would you like to bear your name?"

"The stories," cried Anansi. "The stories that we tell in the forest evening at time when the sun goes down, the stories about Br'er Snake and Br'er Tacumah, Br'er Cow and Br'er Bird and all of us."

Now Tiger liked these stories and he meant to keep them as Tiger stories. He thought to himself, How stupid, how weak this Anansi is. I will play a trick on him so that all the animals will laugh at him. Tiger moved his tail slowly from side to side and said, "Very good, Anansi, very good. I will let the stories be named after you, if you do what I ask."

"Tiger, I will do what you ask."

"Yes, I am sure you will, I am sure you will," said Tiger, moving his tail slowly from side to side. "It is a little thing that I ask. Bring me Mr. Snake alive. Do you know Snake who lives down by the river, Mr. Anansi? Bring him to me alive and you can have the stories."

How do you think Anansi managed to bring back Snake alive?
    Here are some picture clues and a few words to help you make
up the rest of the story.

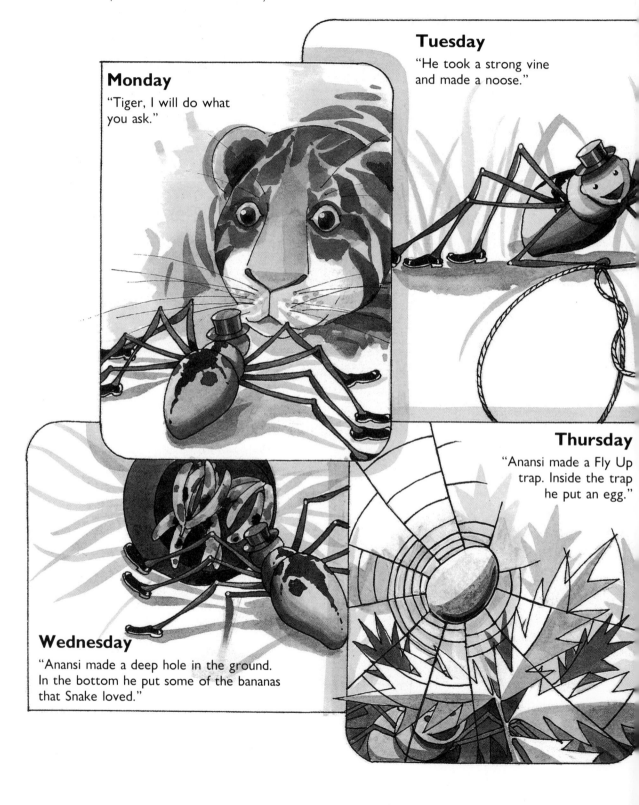

Tuesday

"He took a strong vine
and made a noose."

Monday

"Tiger, I will do what
you ask."

Thursday

"Anansi made a Fly Up
trap. Inside the trap
he put an egg."

Wednesday

"Anansi made a deep hole in the ground.
In the bottom he put some of the bananas
that Snake loved."

Friday

"He sat and thought all day.
It was no use."

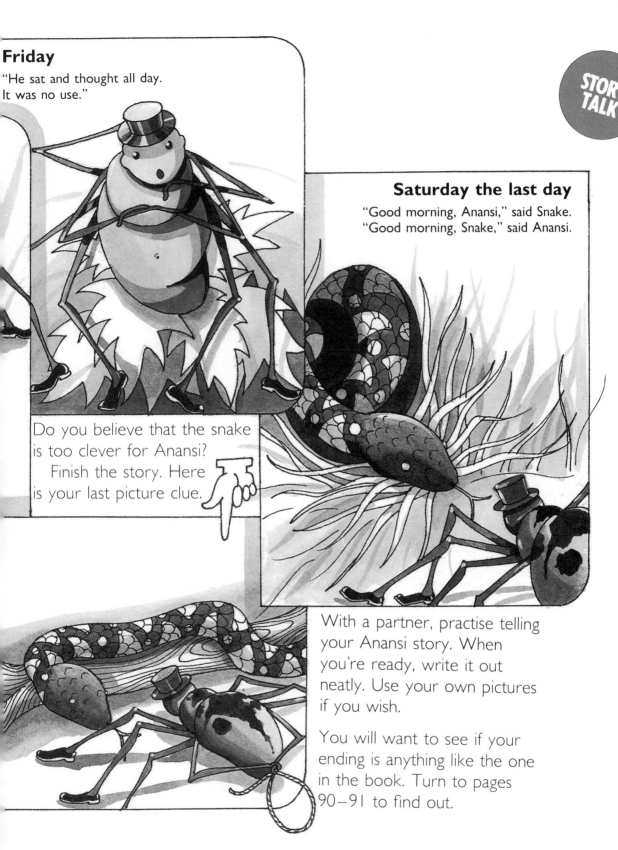

Do you believe that the snake is too clever for Anansi? Finish the story. Here is your last picture clue.

Saturday the last day

"Good morning, Anansi," said Snake.
"Good morning, Snake," said Anansi.

With a partner, practise telling your Anansi story. When you're ready, write it out neatly. Use your own pictures if you wish.

You will want to see if your ending is anything like the one in the book. Turn to pages 90–91 to find out.

THE PERFECT STORYTELLER

What do you think makes a perfect storyteller?
  Talk about it and jot down all your ideas.

Read the story of the king who wanted to become
a perfect storyteller:

There was once a king who liked stories so much that he decided to become a storyteller himself. Since he was the king, however, he would have to be the very best of storytellers, the Perfect Storyteller. So he sent for the finest storytellers in the land and asked them to write him a summary of their art. There were some problems in this, because several couldn't read or write, but when this problem was settled, they set to work and produced a thick book on the subject.

"I haven't time to read all this," said the king. "I asked for a *summary.*" So the storytellers went back to work. At last they returned with a much shorter book, just fifty pages. "Too much!" the king still said. "Summarise! No more than seven sentences. That's all I have time to read."

This time the storytellers didn't know what to do. They considered the matter all ways round and they couldn't think of a short enough summary. They also felt that the king needed to learn a lesson or two if he thought the matter was as simple as that. Eventually they found a solution and they presented it to the king. Written in finest handwriting, seven times over was just one sentence.

"The Perfect Storyteller is the one whose story you remember long after you have forgotten his face."

Find a quiet place and tell this story to yourself out loud. You don't have to use exactly the same words but it will help you if you learn the first and last sentences. Tell the story to someone who has not heard it.

In pairs, write one sentence beginning with the words "The perfect storyteller is . . ."

Write it out neatly for a display in your classroom.

"JUMP" STORIES

One of our sentences for the perfect storyteller went like this:

"The perfect storyteller is someone who can end a story in a way that makes you jump."

This next story in the shape of a poem is a "jump" story — but only if you tell it really well!

Once there was a woman went out to pick beans,
and she found a Hairy Toe.
She took the Hairy Toe home with her,
and that night, when she went to bed,
the wind began to moan and groan.
Away off in the distance
she seemed to hear a voice crying,
"Where's my Hair-r-ry To-o-oe?
Who's got my Hair-r-ry To-o-oe?"

The woman scrooched down,
'way down under the covers,
and about that time
the wind appeared to hit the house,

smoosh,

and the old house creaked and cracked
like something was trying to get in.
The voice had come nearer,
almost at the door now,
and it said,
"Where's my Hair-r-ry To-o-oe?
Who's got my Hair-r-ry To-o-oe?"

66

The woman scrooched further down
under the covers
and pulled them tight around her head.
The wind growled around the house
like some big animal
and r-r-um-umbled
over the chimney.
All at once she heard the door cr-r-a-ack
and Something slipped in
and began to creep over the floor.

The floor went
cre-e-eak, cre-e-eak
at every step that thing took towards her bed.
The woman could almost feel
it bending over her head.
There in an awful voice it said:
"Where's my Hair-r-ry To-o-oe?
Who's got my Hair-r-ry To-o-oe?
You've got it!"

CREAK

CREAK

As a whole class, get ready to tell the story to make another class jump!

After you have read or listened to the poem, look carefully at *sound* and *movement* words.

Make a list of the words which will help you make the story scary. Try out different ways of saying them.

Decide how to share out the poem so that each group has a few lines to learn.

You could tape-record sounds of the wind, doors creaking and footsteps getting closer to make your story more frightening.

Tell or write your own "jump" story. Try it out and see how good it is.

A LETTER FROM A STORY SPINNER

Someone who likes telling "jump" stories when she visits schools is Marion Oughton.

We asked her to write a letter to you.

When I work with children of your age, their first question is usually: "What's that spider's web for?" And I tell them this: as well as being called Marion, I call myself "storyspinner", because I think that I spin stories with words, like spiders spin webs with silk.

Imagine I've come to your school, or you've come to a story session with me in a library, or at a summer play scheme. The first thing you hear is not talking, but music. I play my button accordion . . . After a couple of tunes, I start telling a story.

It might be a spooky story, which I tell very quietly, so everyone is sitting as still as possible, gazing at me, hanging on every word, silent – till I yell the last word and make everyone jump! I love "jump" stories! What I like better than telling them is listening to them. You can tell your own "jump" stories.

Tell your story quietly. It can have scary things in it, like ghosts and skeletons and creaky doors, or it can be very ordinary, about everyday things. But whatever else you do, you must choose that last word carefully. Make sure it has only one syllable (like no, yes, back) or two syllables (like happy, nothing, empty). If it has three syllables (like elephant, nobody, everywhere) or more, the "jump" won't work. And you have to YELL that last word! Have fun with your "jump" stories.

Listening carefully is a big part of storytelling. As the teller or the listener, you have to listen and use your imagination at the same time. If you don't, you lose some of the magic that comes with spinning webs of words.

As well as using your ears when you're telling a story, you need to use your eyes. Look into your audience's eyes, one by one. This helps them to believe the story. Each person believes you're telling it for her, or for him. Try it, next time, and see if the story works better than when you're looking up at the ceiling. I bet it does!

Use your hands too – draw things, point to things. Look at the things you're drawing, and the audience will believe in them.

I can imagine some of you saying: "But I never tell any stories. What's she going on about?" But each one of you is a storyteller. When you go home and tell your mum what a rotten day you had at school – that's a story. When you're telling your best friend about the birthday party you went to on Saturday – that's a story. You could start a storytelling group with your friends at playtime. You could tell stories you've heard, practise your "jump" stories, get your grandad to tell you stories from when he was small and lived somewhere else. You could tape-record your stories, and make illustrations to go with them. There are so many possibilities!

I wish you all the best with your stories, as listeners and as tellers.

A RIDDLE STORY

In groups of three, read this Japanese folk-tale about Taro and his grandmother, re-told by Chia Hearn Chek.

Crops have failed in Taro's village. All the old people have been sent away by the headman because there is not enough food.

Taro hides his grandmother in his house so that she can stay with him.

One day, word went round that there was an important notice up in the market square.

Taro rushed there to see what the matter was.

Presently, he learnt that a poster was put up saying that a big warlord from another village had posed three riddles to his headman to solve. If the headman could not find the answers within three days, the warlord would take away half the land in the village.

However, if he knew the answers, then the warlord would give him all the food he needed.

Taro went home and told his grandmother the news.

"Let me try and solve the riddles," she said.
Taro thought that it was a very good idea.
If she knew the answers, then Taro could ask the headman to allow her to remain in the village.

"Now, listen carefully," Taro said. "Here's the first one. How can you tell which part of a log is nearer the roots and which part nearer the top?"

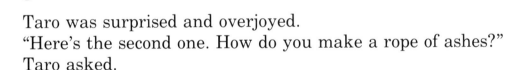

"Put the log in the water. The part nearer the roots will sink while the part nearer the top will float," answered Taro's grandmother.

Taro was surprised and overjoyed.
"Here's the second one. How do you make a rope of ashes?" Taro asked.

"To make a rope of ashes, take a strong rope and pour salt over it. Then burn it slowly," came the answer.
Taro was now a bit excited.

"Here's the third one," Taro continued. "How do you run a thread through a hollow pipe that is curved and crooked?"

The old woman thought for a while and then replied, "Tie a silk thread round an ant's leg. Put some honey at one end and push the ant in at the other end. The ant will reach for the honey and in this way, you will have run the thread through the pipe no matter how crooked and curved it is." She added, "You see, it's all very simple!"

When she had finished saying this, Taro jumped up happily and quickly rushed to the headman's house with the answers to the riddles.

The young headman was astonished at what he heard for there was great wisdom in the answers.

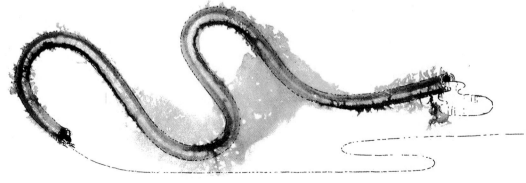

"Tell me, young farmer, did you solve these riddles yourself?" he asked.

"No, my grandmother gave me the answers," Taro replied. When the headman heard this, he was very ashamed of himself for he always thought that old people were useless. The headman thanked Taro and gave him as many gifts as he could carry.

"Your grandmother deserves all these," he said.

Furthermore, the headman at once gave orders that all the old people could return to the village and live there as long as they wished. On that day, there was much rejoicing in the village as old parents were brought together with their children.

From that time onwards, not a single old man or woman was ever sent away from that place.

So peace once again returned to the village. The farmers, now feeling contented, worked harder than ever before. The weather, too, improved and soon there was plenty of food for everyone.

Decide together who will read the parts of the storyteller, Taro and his grandmother.

Try to read the story as if you are telling it to an audience. You will need to practise reading it many times until you know the story and the words well. Then you will be able to look at your listeners as you tell the story, instead of at the pages, and keep them interested.

As a whole class, prepare this story as a play about learning from old people.

Build your play around these scenes:
● the market square;
● Taro's house;
● the headman's house.

One group could mime the action while another group tells the story.

"HOW" STORIES

We make up "how" stories to help us understand the world we live in.

You may have listened to stories about:

How the whale became
How the whale got its throat
How the leopard got its spots
How the crab got its back
How the alphabet was made

and many others.

Here is one you may not know. It is the story of *How Rabbit stole fire*, by Joanna Troughton.

"Hallo, Sky People," said Rabbit. "I have come to teach you a new dance. Look at my dancing hat.

It is a dance to bring the corn from the earth. It is a dance to guide the fish to your nets."

So spoke Rabbit the trickster. And with his words he soothed the Sky People. He charmed them. He flattered them.

They forgot that he was a mischief-maker and welcomed him into their village. "Rabbit shall lead us in the dance!"

75

So Rabbit led the dance! Round and round the fire danced Rabbit. And round and round behind him danced the Sky People. Round and round danced Rabbit, wearing his wonderful head-dress . . .

and as he danced, he bent low to the fire, singing his dancing song. And the Sky People bent low also. Round and round danced Rabbit, and very low he bent . . .

Whoosh! The head-dress was alight!
And away raced Rabbit, out of the
village and down the mountain. "We have been
tricked!" screamed the Sky People. "Rabbit has stolen the
fire!"

On your own, read the story several times until you can remember
what happens – you do not need to remember all the words.

   Tell your story to a friend and help each other to become better
storytellers.

Make up your own "how" story about Rabbit. Remember that Rabbit
is a trickster, and he makes mischief. Here is one idea to start you
thinking:

In the beginning there was no water and the world was dry.
   The Sea People had water but they lived at the bottom of the
ocean and kept it from all other creatures . . .

77

TELLING TALES

Stories were told long before books were written. It is hard to imagine a world without stories. We are telling them to each other most of the time – stories about what we have done, what we have seen, what we have said and what we have heard.

Other people's stories can make us stop and listen. They can make us happy or sad; excited or frightened. They can even make us change our minds.

You probably all know the story of "Little Red Riding Hood". Remind each other of the story. But if the wolf had been telling the story, he might have begun quite differently. Read the beginning of *Little Red Riding Hood, the wolf's story,* by David Henry Wilson.

OK, so I got killed in the end and you all said yippee. I'm not complaining about that. I wasn't as clever as I thought I was, so I'll take my defeat like a wolf. But now that I'm a was-wolf (that is, a dead wolf), and I'm up here in Valhowla (paradise for wolves), I'll rest a lot easier if the record is set straight. The official accounts of what happened that day are all lies, and I hate lies – especially lies about me. So here's the story of what really happened.

In small groups carry on with the wolf's story. Before you begin, think about the answers you could give to these questions:

- What were you doing when you saw Red Riding Hood?
- What did you think when you saw her?
- What did you say to her?
- What did she say to you?
- Why did you go to her grandmother's cottage?
- What happened when you got there?
- Were you frightened when Red Riding Hood arrived?
- Was it true that you pretended to be her grandmother?
- How were you killed?

Tell your story to another group when you have practised it. Try to make them change their minds about what really happened in this story.

Think of other well-known stories that you could re-tell in this kind of way: stories like *Goldilocks and the three bears,*
Hansel and Gretel,
Jack and the beanstalk,
The Pied Piper of Hamelin and
The three Billy Goats Gruff.

Michael Rosen finds another way of
retelling all these tales in his book
Hairy tales and nursery crimes.
Here are the new titles he gives
them: *Goldisocks and the wee bears,*
Handsel and Gristle,
Jack and the tinstalk,
The Fried Pepper of Hamelin.
Turn over the page to meet *The Silly Ghosts Gruff.*

THE SILLY GHOSTS GRUFF

Once there were three ghosts. They were called the Silly Ghosts Gruff. There was Little Silly Ghost Gruff, Big Silly Ghost Gruff and Piddle-sized Silly Ghost Gruff.

And they all lived in a field by a river. One day they thought they would like to cross the river to eat the grass on the other side.

Now, over this river there was a fridge and underneath the fridge was a horrible roll. A horrible Cheese roll. So the Little Silly Ghost Gruff, he stepped on to the fridge, drip, drop, drip, drop, over the fridge; when suddenly, there on the fridge was the horrible roll.

"I'm a roll-fol-de-roll and you'll eat me for your supper!"

"Oh no, oh no, oh no," said the Little Silly Ghost Gruff. "I don't want to eat you. My big brother the Piddle-sized Silly Ghost Gruff is going to be coming along soon and he can eat you for his supper."

"Very well," said the horrible roll, "you can cross the fridge."

And drip, drop, drip, drop, over the fridge went the Little Silly Ghost Gruff.

Next to come along was the Piddle-sized Silly Ghost Gruff.

Drip, drop, drip, drop, over the fridge he came until suddenly, there

in front of him, on the fridge, was the horrible roll.

"I'm a roll-fol-de-roll and you'll eat me for your supper."

"Oh no, oh no, no, no," said the Piddle-sized Silly Ghost Gruff. "I don't want to eat you. My big brother, the Big Silly Ghost Gruff is coming soon and he can eat you for his supper."

"Very well," said the roll, "you can cross the fridge."
And drip, drop, drip, drop, the Piddle-sized Silly Ghost Gruff crossed the fridge to the other side.

Then along comes the Big Silly Ghost Gruff. Drip, drop, drip, drop, over the fridge and, suddenly, there was the horrible roll again.

"I'm a roll-fol-de-roll and you'll eat me for your supper."

"Oh can I? Oh can I?" said the Big Silly Ghost Gruff.
And at that he ran at the horrible roll and went straight through it (he was a ghost, don't forget).

And so over the fridge he went drip, drop, drip, drop, till he got to the other side.

And from that day on, no roll, no cheese roll, or ham roll or even a jam roll ever bothered the Silly Ghosts Gruff ever again.

First, try out different ways of reading *The Silly Ghosts Gruff* aloud in small groups.

Then, find a copy of *The three Billy Goats Gruff.*

When you have read this story aloud, talk about the changes Michael Rosen has made. Which version of the story do you prefer?

THE HORRIBLE STORY

Can you remember being scared by stories like *The three Billy Goats Gruff* when you were little?

Talk about some of these stories and why they frightened you.

In this next story, by Margaret Mahy, Robert and Allan decide to frighten Robert's little brother, Christopher. They plan to tell him a horrible story . . .

Read what happens.

Outside it was quite dark, but inside the boys had a candle-lantern which cast a pale, flickering light on the tawny sides of the tent. You could not see much – only the long shapes of sleeping-bags and blankets, and the humpy shapes of heads and pillows.

The two longest shapes were Robert and Allan, who were by the door flap, which was fastened back tonight. They had told Christopher, Robert's little brother, that they wanted to look out into the garden and watch the stars, but really they had their own secret reasons for wanting to be together by the door, and for making him sleep on his own at the back of the tent. *His* bedtime shape was just blankets, for he had no sleeping-bag, and it was a shorter shape than Allan's or Robert's, because he was only small – not quite seven – and they were ten.

Yesterday morning there had been no tent. A large parcel had arrived at lunch time addressed to Mr Robert and Mr Christopher Johnson. Robert's eyes had shone with surprise and delight when it had been opened, and its layers of paper and cardboard peeled back. It was a tent – not just a white tent such as you might see in any camp-ground either, but a tawny-brown tent that could belong to an Indian or an outlaw or some wild, fierce hero.

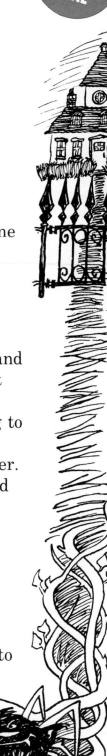

There had been the fun of fitting the poles together and putting it up at the bottom of the garden, sheltered by the hedge, and the sudden excitement when they realized that they would be allowed to sleep out all night in it.

"Can Allan come too, Mum?" asked Robert, because Allan was his best friend, and they always shared adventures.

"Of course he may, if he is allowed," Mother replied, smiling.

"Me too!" Christopher cried anxiously, for he knew that when Allan and Robert were together he was always just a little brother to be left behind or taken no notice of. "It's *my* tent too, isn't it?"

Robert looked at him rather sourly. He said, "You can come some other time. You've got lots of chances."

His mother turned round sharply.

"Now, don't be difficult, Bob!" she said. "Of course Christopher can camp out too. If there's no room for Christopher there's no room for Allan either."

So here they were, the three of them, Allan and Robert, and Christopher on his own in the back of the tent, looking a bit lonely and small in the flickering shadows.

Secretly Allan nudged Robert as a sign that he was going to begin the Get-rid-of-Christopher plan . . . a plan they had made that afternoon riding their bicycles home from the river.

"Little kids get scared easy as easy in the dark," Allan had said . . . "I bet when your little brother hears one of my famous horrible tales he'll run inside to Mummy and won't want to come into the tent ever again. Then we'll have a midnight feast, eh? I'll bring a tin of fruit salad, and a tin opener, and some luncheon sausage."

"I'll buy a packet of biscuits," Robert had replied. "I've got ten pence."

As he remembered this he slid his hand under the pillow to feel the biscuits he'd hidden there. The paper crackled, and

Christopher turned his head a little bit. Quickly Robert nudged Allan to show that he understood the plan was beginning. Allan blew out the candle in the lantern and for a moment everything went black as the night came, silent and sudden, into the tent.

"Hey," said Allan, "I know a story. It's pretty ghostly though . . ." He let his voice fade away uncertainly.

"Go on!" Robert said. "Tell us! I'm not scared."

"I'm not scared either," said Christopher's piping voice from the back of the tent. He did not sound the least bit like a wild, fierce hero though.

"It's good you're not scared," Allan declared, "because it's a really horrible story, and it's about a boy called Christopher too. Now listen!

"This boy called Christopher lived in an old, dark house on the edge of a big forest. The forest was old too, and dark, like this tent, and full of creepy noises. Sometimes people went in, but no one ever came out again. Lots of rats lived in this forest, big as cats . . ." Allan paused, thinking out the next bit. In the little silence Robert was amazed to hear Christopher's small voice come in unexpectedly.

"When those rats ran around," he said, "their feet made a rustly sound, didn't they?" Outside, the hedge rustled in the wind, and Christopher added, ". . . a bit like that."

"Huh!" said Allan crossly. "And I suppose you think you know what else lived in the forest?"

"Yes . . . yes, I do, Allan."

"Look, who's telling this story?" cried Allan indignantly. Then he asked rather cautiously, "Well, what else *did* live there?"

"Spiders," said Christopher. "Big hairy spiders . . . big as footballs . . . but hairy all over like dish mops, huge black dish mops going scuttle, scuttle on lots of thin legs –"

Allan interrupted him fiercely. "Hey shut *up*, will you! This

84

is my story, isn't it? Well then . . . there weren't any spiders, but there was a dragon."

Allan went on talking about the bigness and smokiness of the dragon, but Robert felt disappointed in it. Somehow it did not seem nearly as frightening as the scuttling, hairy spiders. On the other side of the tent something went *tap, tap, tap!* like quick little feet running over the canvas. Allan stopped and listened.

"It's just the wind," Christopher said in a kind voice. "It's just a scraping, twiggy piece from the hedge. Go on, Allan."

Robert suddenly felt sorry for Christopher, lying there so trustingly staring into the dark with round black eyes like shoe buttons. Christopher was just not an adventurer. He was . . . the sort who would rather stay at home and read fairy stories than plan wars in the gorse or battle over the sand hills. Perhaps it was a bit mean to frighten him out of the tent, a tent which was really half his.

"Never mind!" thought Robert. "He'll have lots of other chances." Under his pillow the biscuit paper crackled faintly.

"And then, one night . . ." Allan said mysteriously, "the little boy was on his own in the old house when . . . guess what happened?"

"Somebody knocked at the door," said Christopher promptly. "Three knocks, very slowly, KNOCK KNOCK KNOCK . . ."

"Fair go!" replied Allan scornfully. "Do you know who it was, Mr Smart?"

"Yes," Christopher went on, "the little boy opened the door and there was a man there all in black, at least it looked like a man, but you couldn't tell really, because he had a black thing over his face, a black silk scarf thing. And do you know what he said? He said, 'Little boy, the time has come for you to follow *me*.'" Christopher stopped, and the tent was quiet except for the sad-sea sound of the wind.

"Did the boy go?" asked Robert. He did not want to ask, but

suddenly he felt he had to know. Allan said nothing. Christopher's voice was almost dreamy, as he replied,

"Yes, he did. He just couldn't help it. And as he went out of the door it shut itself behind him. The gate did too. Then they were in that forest. Everywhere was the rustling noise of rats and spiders."

"Hey . . ." began Allan.

"What?" squeaked Christopher.

"Nothing! Go on!" Allan said.

"And *things* followed them," Christopher went on, making his voice deep and mysterious. "The man went first, and the boy followed the man, and if he looked back he saw things with *eyes* coming after him, but he couldn't see what things they were."

"What were they?" asked Robert in a small voice.

"Just things!" said Christopher solemnly. "Spooky things . . . with little red eyes," he added thoughtfully. "Then they came to a clearing place – there was a fire burning – not a yellow fire though, a blue one. All the flames were blue. It looked *ghastly!*" cried Christopher, pleased with his grown-up word. "There were three heads – just heads, no arms or legs or bodies or anything – sticking out of the ground round the fire." He stopped again. Allan and Robert could hear their own breathing. They did not ask any questions and Christopher went on with his story again. "They were ugly, UGLY heads and they had these smiles on their faces" – Christopher was trying to think of words bad enough to describe the smiles – "more horrible than anything you ever saw. They were yellow too, mind you, like cheese. One head looked at the man with cruel, mean eyes and said,

"'So you brought us some food.'

"The man replied, 'Yes, and it's very tender tonight.'

"'Well, it's just as well,' the head said, 'or we'd have had to eat *you*.'

"Then the second head said, 'We'll have a good tuck-in tonight, eh, brothers? Bags I be the one to drink his blood.' Then the third head opened its mouth, wide as wide, like a cat yawning, you know, and it had all these pointy teeth, like needles, some short and some long, and it didn't even say anything. It just began to scream, horrible, high-up screams . . .'"

Christopher's voice got louder and higher with excitement, and at this very moment, almost it seemed at Robert's ear, a shrill furious howl arose from under the hedge. Allan scrambled to his feet with a cry of terror and went hopping madly out of the tent, too frightened to get out of his sleeping-bag first.

"The head!" yelled Robert and followed him, so frightened he felt sick and shaky in his stomach. Under the hedge were heads with teeth like needles waiting to bite him up as if he was an apple.

Christopher was alone in the tent. Quickly he hopped from under his blankets and stuck his head out through the tent flap. He saw Allan and Robert, still zipped in their sleeping-bags, hopping and stumbling up the lawn.

"It ends happily!" he shouted.

Then he thoughtfully put his hand under Allan's pillow and helped himself to the luncheon sausage hidden there.

Voices were talking on the veranda.

"It was only a cat fight!" Christopher's father was saying. "Great Scott, if you're going to be scared by a cat fight, we'll never make campers of you."

Christopher grinned to himself in the dark and quietly felt for the biscuits under Robert's pillow.

In pairs, make up your own horrible stories, each with a surprise ending.

Practise telling your stories in a scary way.

87

CAMPING OUT

In this poem by Vernon Scannell, Peter is given a tent for his ninth birthday present. He is keen to spend his first night in the tent. His father warns him that he might feel afraid out in the dark field all alone.

Peter has no fear of darkness until . . .

His birthday fell in mid-July,
A golden season filled with trees,
Green cauldrons bubbling in the sky
With songs of birds, and, on the breeze
Like airborne petals, butterflies
Signalled, "Peter now is nine!"

That morning brought a great surprise
Which sent a thrill along his spine
And filled his heart with wordless joy:
His parents gave to him a tent,
A gift that almost any boy
Would welcome, but to him it meant
A dream had wakened into fact –
For months he'd longed to spend a night
Under canvas; all he lacked
Had in a second been put right
When he unpacked his birthday present.
"I'll camp in Coppin's field tonight."
His father smiled: "It sounds quite pleasant,
That field's a perfect camping site.
But Peter, out there in the dark
You might be frightened, all alone.
Just now the whole thing seems a lark
But night has terrors of its own."

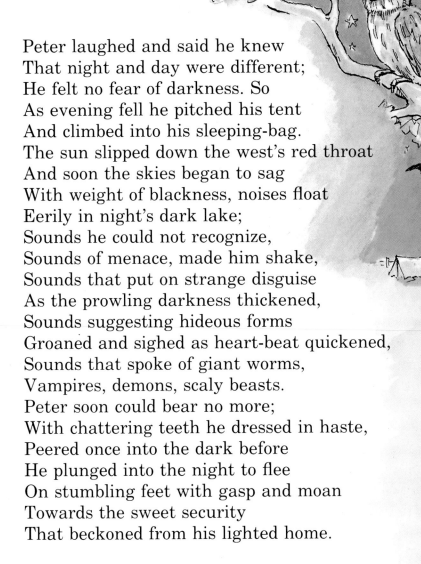

Peter laughed and said he knew
That night and day were different;
He felt no fear of darkness. So
As evening fell he pitched his tent
And climbed into his sleeping-bag.
The sun slipped down the west's red throat
And soon the skies began to sag
With weight of blackness, noises float
Eerily in night's dark lake;
Sounds he could not recognize,
Sounds of menace, made him shake,
Sounds that put on strange disguise
As the prowling darkness thickened,
Sounds suggesting hideous forms
Groaned and sighed as heart-beat quickened,
Sounds that spoke of giant worms,
Vampires, demons, scaly beasts.
Peter soon could bear no more;
With chattering teeth he dressed in haste,
Peered once into the dark before
He plunged into the night to flee
On stumbling feet with gasp and moan
Towards the sweet security
That beckoned from his lighted home.

Work in pairs. One of you is Peter, the other one is Peter's mother.
Make up the conversation they have when Peter runs into his home
away from his tent in the field.

At school next day, Peter's friend asks him what he got for his
birthday. Make up the story Peter tells about his night in the tent.

Tell or write your own story about a time when you felt really brave
until . . . you became very scared!

89

FROM TIGER TO ANANSI

This is the end of the story which began on page 60.

"Good morning, Anansi," said Snake.

"Good morning, Snake," said Anansi.

"Anansi, I am very angry with you. You have been trying to catch me all week. You set a Fly Up to catch me. The day before you made a Slippery Hole for me. The day before that you made a Calaban. I have a good mind to kill you, Anansi."

"Ah, you are too clever, Snake," said Anansi. "You are much too clever. Yes, what you say is so. I tried to catch you, but I failed. Now I can never prove that you are the longest animal in the world, longer even than the bamboo tree."

"Of course I am the longest of all animals," cried Snake. "I am much longer than the bamboo tree."

"What, longer than that bamboo tree across there?" asked Anansi.

"Of course I am," said Snake. "Look and see." Snake came out of the hole and stretched himself out at full length.

"Yes, you are very, very long," said Anansi, "but the bamboo tree is very long, too. Now that I look at you and at the bamboo tree I must say that the bamboo tree seems longer. But it's hard to say because it is further away."

"Well, bring it nearer," cried Snake. "Cut it down and put it beside me. You will soon see that I am much longer."

Anansi ran to the bamboo tree and cut it down. He placed it on the ground and cut off all its branches. Bush, bush, bush, bush! There it was, long and straight as a flagstaff.

"Now put it beside me," said Snake.

Anansi put the long bamboo tree down on the ground beside Snake. Then he said:

"Snake, when I go up to see where your head is, you will

crawl up. When I go down to see where your tail is, you will crawl down. In that way you will always seem to be longer than the bamboo tree, which really is longer than you are."

"Tie my tail, then!" said Snake. "Tie my tail! I know that I am longer than the bamboo, whatever you say."

Anansi tied Snake's tail to the end of the bamboo. Then he ran up to the other end.

"Stretch, Snake, stretch, and we will see who is longer."

A crowd of animals were gathering round. Here was something better than a race. "Stretch, Snake, stretch," they called.

Snake stretched as hard as he could. Anansi tied him round his middle so that he should not slip back. Now one more try. Snake knew that if he stretched hard enough he would prove to be longer than the bamboo.

Anansi ran up to him. "Rest yourself for a little, Snake, and then stretch again. If you can stretch another six inches you will be longer than the bamboo. Try your hardest. Stretch so that you even have to shut your eyes. Ready?"

"Yes," said Snake. Then Snake made a mighty effort. He stretched so hard that he had to squeeze his eyes shut. "Hooray!" cried the animals. "You are winning, Snake. Just two inches more."

And at that moment Anansi tied Snake's head to the bamboo. There he was. At last he had caught Snake, all by himself.

The animals fell silent. Yes, there Snake was, all tied up, ready to be taken to Tiger. And feeble Anansi had done this. They could laugh at him no more.

And never again did Tiger dare to call these stories by his name. They were Anansi stories for ever after, from that day to this.

Practise reading the whole story aloud. Give each creature a different voice. Try to find other Anansi stories to share with your friends.

91

THE DIARY OF A CHURCH MOUSE

At the beginning of this book you met Humphrey, the other church mice and Supercat Sampson. You will be pleased to learn that Sampson escaped from his "catnappers" and that Humphrey kept up his diary. Here are his entries from the month of December.

In pairs, take turns to read Humphrey's diary.

1st December   Everybody's saying how much they hate Christmas but as the children love it so much they're prepared to put up with having a week off work and staying in bed late and eating twice as much as usual just for their sake.

2nd December   Myself I think a bit of Christmas Spirit is quite a good thing. So does Arthur and a few others so we're going to go carol singing just to spread some of it around Wortlethorpe.

3rd–8th December   Practising carols in the vestry. We weren't very good at first but now, if we really try, we all get to the end of even the longest carol within seconds of each other. So tomorrow night we'll go out and start spreading the Christmas Spirit.

9th December   No more Christmas Spirit spreading for me, I can tell you. We went out in the evening and even though Sampson insisted on tagging along we were brimming over with Christmas Spirit. At the first likely-looking house we came to we let fly with "The First Noel". Blow me if Sampson didn't join in. Well, that did it. It was jolly nearly our last Noel. If we hadn't got back to the vestry in double-quick time we'd have frozen to death. Me and Sampson no longer have anything to say to each other.

10th December   We've been planning our Christmas party. Everybody just assumes that Father Christmas will show up but they should know by now that you really can't rely on him. I shall have to be prepared to fill the gap.

11th–14th December Making a suit like Father Christmas's just in case. Found a nice secret place behind the altar to work.

16th December In the organ loft there's a large box full of Smarties and peanuts and dolly mixtures and jelly babies and things that the choir master has confiscated during choir practice. I tested them thoroughly for flavour and as they were all right I borrowed some. They'll make lovely presents if F.C. doesn't come. Feeling rather sick. I think I'll go to bed early.

18th–21st December Finished suit, it looks really good. I hope F.C. doesn't show up. It would be a shame for all this work to be wasted.

22nd December We all went out collecting Christmas decorations. It was nice but a bit dangerous.

23rd December We spent the whole day putting up Christmas decorations.

24th December We had the party today and what a shambles it was. Father Christmas didn't show up, just as I'd expected, so at about six o'clock I went and put my F.C. suit on. When I got back the place was crawling with Father Christmases! If people didn't go doing things behind other people's backs we wouldn't get into messes like this. Now all the kids are going to think that there's fifty-seven Father Christmases and expect fifty-seven presents every Christmas.

25th December Another Christmas Day. Had a huge breakfast, slept all morning. Stupendous dinner, slept all afternoon. Colossal tea, slept all evening. Gigantic supper, couldn't sleep a wink all night.

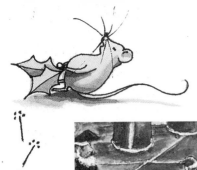

Talk about some of the things that made you laugh. Plan and write Humphrey's diary for the rest of December. Think about some of the things that could happen between Christmas and New Year – the mice and Sampson might go to see the pantomime "Puss in Boots", for example.

Read again Humphrey's kite-flying episode on pages 4–7.

Write a few entries for Humphrey's diary about some days in summer and at Harvest Festival time.

95

ACKNOWLEDGEMENTS

The authors and publishers are grateful to the following for permission to reproduce previously published material: Andersen Press Ltd. for illustrations and text from *Two monsters* by David McKee, Arrow Books Ltd; A & C Black (Publishers) Ltd. for "The dragon of death" from *Nightmares* by Jack Prelutsky, 1978; Blackie and Son Ltd. for illustrations and text from *Taro and his grandmother* re-told by Chia Hearn Chek, 1975, and *How Rabbit stole fire* by Joanna Troughton, 1979; The Bodley Head for an illustration from *Up and Up,* written and illustrated by Shirley Hughes, 1979; extracts from 'Petronella' in *The practical princess and other liberating fairy tales* by Jay Williams, and *Letters for Lettie* by John Agard; Jonathan Cape Ltd. for illustrations from *Would you rather ...?,* written and illustrated by John Burningham; J. M. Dent & Sons Ltd. for 'The Horrible Story' from *The second Margaret Mahy story book* by Margaret Mahy and material from *There's a wolf in my pudding* by David Henry Wilson, 1986; Andre Deutsch Ltd. for an illustration from *One moonlit night* by David Armitage, 1983, and an extract from *The battle of Bubble and Squeak* by Philippa Pearce, 1978; Victor Gollancz Ltd. for illustrations, including the cover illustration, and text from *Tumbleweed,* written by Dick King-Smith and illustrated by Ian Newsham, 1987; Hamish Hamilton Ltd. for illustrations and text from *A walk in the park* by Anthony Browne, 1986; Macmillan Publishers Ltd. for illustrations and text from *Henry's Quest,*1986, *Diary of a Church Mouse* and *Church Mouse in action,* written and illustrated by Graham Oakley; and an extract from *Anansi, the spider man* by Philip Sherlock; Methuen Children's Books for illustrations from *The knight and the dragon* by Tomie de Paola; Leslie Norris for "Bird and Boy" from *Norris's Ark,* Tidal Press, Cranberry Isles, Maine and "Boy Flying"; Marion Oughton for her letter to children; Vernon Scannell for "Camping Out".

Every effort has been made to trace all the copyright holders, but if any have been inadvertently overlooked the publishers will be pleased to make the necessary arrangement at the first opportunity.

Illustrations: Russ Billington pages 33, 38, 39, 74, 75, 76, 77; Irene Inness pages 12, 13, 14, 15, 16, 17; Hilary McElderry pages 50, 51, 53, 55, 56, 57, 58, 59; Jenny Mumford pages 23, 44, 45, 46, 47, 48, 66, 67, 88, 89; Frank Nichols pages 20, 21, 22, 24, 25, 27, 28; Cathie Shuttleworth pages 60, 61, 62, 63, 90, 91, 92, 93, 94, 95; Joyce Smith pages 64, 65. Cover illustration: Lynne Willey. Contents page: Frank Nichols.

Thomas Nelson and Sons Ltd
Nelson House   Mayfield Road
Walton-on-Thames   Surrey
KT12 5PL   UK

51 York Place
Edinburgh
EH1 3JD   UK

Thomas Nelson (Hong Kong) Ltd
Toppan Building 10/F
22A Westlands Road
Quarry Bay   Hong Kong

Thomas Nelson Australia
102 Dodds Street
South Melbourne
Victoria 3205   Australia

Nelson Canada
1120 Birchmount Road
Scarborough   Ontario
M1K 5G4   Canada

© Sheila Freeman and Esther Munns 1990

First published by Macmillan Education Ltd 1990
ISBN 0-333-45389-1

This edition published by Thomas Nelson and Sons Ltd 1992

ISBN 0-17-422729-9
NPN 9 8 7 6 5 4 3 2

Printed in Hong Kong